MW00635717

THE PICKERING MANUSCRIPT

William Blake

Table of Contents

THE PICKERING MANUSCRIPT

William Blake

Kessinger Publishing reprints thousands of hard–to–find books!

Visit us at http://www.kessinger.net

- The Smile
- The Golden Net
- The Mental Traveller
- The Land of Dreams
- Mary
- The Crystal Cabinet
- The Grey Monk
- Auguries of Innocence
- Long John Brown and Little Mary Bell
- William Bond

The Smile

There is a smile of love,
And there is a smile of deceit,
And there is a smile of smiles
In which these two smiles meet.

And there is a frown of hate,
And there is a frown of disdain,
And there is a frown of frowns
Which you strive to forget in vain,

For it sticks in the heart's deep core
And it sticks in the deep backbone—
And no smile that ever was smil'd,
But only one smile alone,

That betwixt the cradle and grave
It only once smil'd can be;
And, when it once is smil'd,
There's an end to all misery.

The Golden Net

Three Virgins at the break of day:
`Whither, young man, whither away
Alas for woe! alas for woe!'
They cry, and tears for ever flow.
The one was cloth'd in flames of fire,
The other cloth'd in iron wire,
The other cloth'd in tears and sighs
Dazzling bright before my eyes.
They bore a Net of golden twine
To hang upon the branches fine.
Pitying I wept to see the woe
That Love and Beauty undergo,
To be consum'd in burning fires
And in ungratified desires,
And in tears cloth'd night and day
Melted all my soul away.
When they saw my tears, a smile
That did Heaven itself beguile,
Bore the Golden Net aloft
As on downy pinions soft,
Over the Morning of my day.
Underneath the net I stray,
Now entreating Burning Fire
Now entreating Iron Wire,
Now entreating Tears and Sighs—
O! when will the morning rise?

The Mental Traveller

I travell'd thro' a land of men,
A land of men and women too;
And heard and saw such dreadful things
As cold earth-wanderers never knew.

For there the Babe is born in joy
That was begotten in dire woe;
Just as we reap in joy the fruit
Which we in bitter tears did sow.

And if the Babe is born a boy
He's given to a Woman Old,
Who nails him down upon a rock,
Catches his shrieks in cups of gold.

She binds iron thorns around his head,
She pierces both his hands and feet,
She cuts his heart out at his side,
To make it feel both cold and heat.

Her fingers number every nerve,
Just as a miser counts his gold;
She lives upon his shrieks and cries,
And she grows young as he grows old.

Till he becomes a bleeding Youth,
And she becomes a Virgin bright;
Then he rends up his manacles,
And binds her down for his delight.

He plants himself in all her nerves,

Just as a husbandman his mould;
And she becomes his dwelling–place
And garden fruitful seventyfold.

And aged Shadow, soon he fades,
Wandering round an earthly cot,
Full filled all with gems and gold
Which he by industry had got.

And these are the gems of the human soul,
The rubies and pearls of a love–sick eye,
The countless gold of the aching heart,
The martyr's groan and the lover's sigh.

They are his meat, they are his drink
He feeds the beggar and the poor
And the wayfaring traveller:
For ever open in his door.

His grief is their eternal joy;
They make the roofs and walls to ring;
Till from the fire on the hearth
A little Female Babe does spring.

And she is all of solid fire
And gems and gold, that none his hand
Dares stretch to touch her baby form,
Or wrap her in his swaddling–band.

But she comes to the man she loves,
If young or old, or rich or poor;
They soon drive out the Aged Host,
A beggar at another's door.

He wanders weeping far away,
Until some other take him in;

Oft blind and age–bent, sore distrest,
Until he can a Maiden win.

And to allay his freezing age,
The poor man takes her in his arms;
The cottage fades before his sight,
The garden and its lovely charms.

The guests are scatter'd thro' the land,
For the eye altering alters all;
The senses roll themselves in fear,
And the flat earth becomes a ball;

The stars, sun, moon, all shrink away
A desert vast without a bound,
And nothing left to eat or drink,
And a dark desert all around.

The honey of her infant lips,
The bread and wine of her sweet smile,
The wild game of her roving eye,
Does him to infancy beguile;

For as he eats and drinks he grows
Younger and younger every day;
And on the desert wild they both
Wander in terror and dismay.

Like the wild stage she flees away,
Her fear plants many a thicket wild;
While he pursues her night and day,
By various arts of love beguil'd;

By various arts of love and hate,
Till the wide desert planted o'er
With labyrinths of wayward love,

Where roam the lion, wolf, and boar.

Till he becomes a wayward Babe,
And she a weeping Woman Old.
Then many a lover wanders here;
The sun and stars are nearer roll'd;

The trees bring forth sweet ecstasy
To all who in the desert roam;
Till many a city there is built,
And many a pleasant shepherd's home.

But when they find the Frowning Babe,
Terror strikes thro' the region wide:
They cry `The Babe! the Babe is born!'
And flee away on every side.

For who dare touch the Frowning Form,
His arm is wither'd to its root;
Lions, boars, wolves, all howling flee,
And every tree does shed its fruit.

And none can touch that Frowning Form,
Except it be a Woman Old;
She nails him down upon the rock,
And all is done as I have told.

The Land of Dreams

Awake, awake, my little boy!
Thou wast thy mother's only joy;
Why dost thou weep in thy gentle sleep?
Awake! thy father does thee keep.

`O, what land is the Land of Dreams?
What are its mountains, and what are its streams?
O father! I saw my mother there,
Among the lilies by waters fair.

`Among the lambs, clothed in white,
She walk'd with her Thomas in sweet delight.
I wept for joy, like a dove I mourn;
O! when shall I again return?'

Dear child, I also by pleasant streams
Have wander'd all night in the Land of Dreams;
But tho' calm and warm the waters wide,
I could not get to the other side.

`Father, O father! what do we here
In this land of unbelief and fear?
The Land of Dreams is better far,
Above the light of the morning star.'

Mary

Sweet Mary, the first time she ever was there,
Came into the ball–room among the fair;
The young men and maidens around her throng,
And these are the words upon every tongue;

`An Angel is here from the heavenly climes,
Or again does return the golden times;
Her eyes outshine every brilliant ray,
She opens her lips—'tis the Month of May.'

Mary moves in soft beauty and conscious delight,
To augment with sweet smiles all the joys of the night,
Nor once blushes to own to the rest of the fair
That sweet Love and Beauty are worthy our care.

In the morning the villagers rose with delight,
And repeated with pleasure the joys of the night,
And Mary arose among friends to be free,
But no friend from henceforward thou, Mary, shalt see.

Some said she was proud, some call'd her a whore,
And some, when she passed by, shut to the door;
A damp cold came o'er her, her blushes all fled;
Her lilies and roses are blighted and shed.

`O, why was I born with a different face?
Why was I not born like this envious race?
Why did Heaven adorn me with bountiful hand,
And then set me down in an envious land?

`To be weak as a lamb and smooth as a dove,

THE PICKERING MANUSCRIPT

And not to raise envy, is call'd Christian love;
But if you raise envy your merit's to blame
For planting such spite in the weak and the tame.

`I will humble my beauty, I will not dress fine,
I will keep from the ball, and my eyes shall not shine;
And if any girl's lover forsakes her for me
I'll refuse him my hand, and from envy be free.'

She went out in morning attir'd plain and neat;
`Proud Mary's gone mad,' said the child in the street;
She went out in morning in plain neat attire,
And came home in evening bespatter'd with mire.

She trembled and wept, sitting on the bedside,
She forgot it was night, and she trembled and cried;
She forgot it was night, she forgot it was morn,
Her soft memory imprinted with faces of scorn;

With faces of scorn and with eyes of disdain,
Like foul fiends inhabiting Mary's mild brain;
She remembers no face like the Human Divine,
All faces have envy, sweet Mary, but thine;

And thine is a face of sweet love in despair,
And thine is a face of mild sorrow and care,
And thine is a face of wild terror and fear
That shall never be quiet till laid on its bier.

The Crystal Cabinet

The Maiden caught me in the wild,
Where I was dancing merrily;
She put me into her Cabinet,
And lock'd me up with a golden key.

This Cabinet is form'd of gold
And pearl and crystal shining bright,
And within it opens into a world
And a little lovely moony night.

Another England there I saw,
Another London with its Tower,
Another Thames and other hills,
And another pleasant Surrey bower,

Another Maiden like herself,
Translucent, lovely, shining clear,
Threefold each in the other clos'd—
O, what a pleasant trembling fear!

O, what a smile! a threefold smile
Fill'd me, that like a flame I burn'd;
I bent to kiss the lovely Maid,
And found a threefold kiss return'd.

I strove to seize the inmost form
With ardour fierce and hands of flame,
But burst the Crystal Cabinet,
And like a weeping Babe became—

A weeping Babe upon the wild,

And weeping Woman pale reclin'd,
And in the outward air again
I fill'd with woes the passing wind.

The Grey Monk

`I die, I die!' the Mother said,
`My children die for lack of bread.
What more has the merciless tyrant said?'
The Monk sat down on the stony bed.

The blood red ran from the Grey Monk's side,
His hands and feet were wounded wide,
His body bent, his arms and knees
Like to the roots of ancient trees.

His eye was dry; no tear could flow:
A hollow groan first spoke his woe.
He trembled and shudder'd upon the bed;
At length with a feeble cry he said:

`When God commanded this hand to write
In the studious hours of deep midnight,
He told me the writing I wrote should prove
The bane of all that on Earth I love.

`My brother starv'd between two walls,
His children's cry my soul appalls;
I mock'd at the wrack and griding chain,
My bent body mocks their torturing pain.

`Thy father drew his sword in the North,
With his thousands strong he marched forth;
Thy brother has arm'd himself in steel,
To avenge the wrongs thy children feel.

`But vain the sword and vain the bow,

They never can work War's overthrow.
The hermit's prayer and the widow's tear
Alone can free the world from fear.

`For a tear is an intellectual thing,
And a sigh is the sword of an Angel King,
And the bitter groan of the martyr's woe
Is an arrow from the Almighty's bow.

`The hand of Vengeance found the bed
To which the purple tyrant fled;
The iron hand crush'd the tyrant's head,
And became a tyrant in his stead.'

Auguries of Innocence

To see a World in a grain of sand,
And a Heaven in a wild flower,
Hold Infinity in the palm of your hand,
And Eternity in an hour.
A robin redbreast in a cage
Puts all Heaven in a rage.
A dove–house fill'd with doves and pigeons
Shudders Hell thro' all its regions.
A dog starv'd at his master's gate
Predicts the ruin of the State.
A horse misus'd upon the road
Calls to Heaven for human blood.
Each outcry of the hunted hare
A fibre from the brain does tear.
A skylark wounded in the wing,
A cherubim does cease to sing.
The game–cock clipt and arm'd for fight
Does the rising sun affright.
Every wolf's and lion's howl
Raises from Hell a Human soul.
The wild deer, wandering here and there,
Keeps the Human soul from care.
The lamb misus'd breeds public strife,
And yet forgives the butcher's knife.
The bat that flits at close of eve
Has left the brain that won't believe.
The owl that calls upon the night
Speaks the unbeliever's fright.
He who shall hurt the little wren
Shall never be belov'd by men.
He who the ox to wrath has mov'd

Shall never be by woman lov'd.
The wanton boy that kills the fly
Shall feel the spider's enmity.
He who torments the chafer's sprite
Weaves a bower in endless night.
The caterpillar on the leaf
Repeats to thee thy mother's grief.
Kill not the moth nor butterfly,
For the Last Judgement draweth nigh.
He who shall train the horse to war
Shall never pass the polar bar.
The beggar's dog and widow's cat,
Feed them, and thou wilt grow fat.
The gnat that sings his summer's song
Poison gets from Slander's tongue.
The poison of the snake and newt
Is the sweat of Envy's foot.
The poison of the honey–bee
Is the artist's jealousy.
The prince's robes and beggar's rags
Are toadstools on the miser's bags.
A truth that's told with bad intent
Beats all the lies you can invent.
It is right it should be so;
Man was made for joy and woe;
And when this we rightly know,
Thro' the world we safely go.
Joy and woe are woven fine,
A clothing for the soul divine;
Under every grief and pine
Runs a joy with silken twine.
The babe is more than swaddling–bands;
Throughout all these human lands
Tools were made, and born were hands,
Every farmer understands.
Every tear from every eye

Becomes a babe in Eternity;
This is caught by Females bright,
And return'd to its own delight.
The bleat, the bark, bellow, and roar
Are waves that beat on Heaven's shore.
The babe that weeps the rod beneath
Writes revenge in realms of death.
The beggar's rags, fluttering in air,
Does to rags the heavens tear.
The soldier, arm'd with sword and gun,
Palsied strikes the summer's sun.
The poor man's farthing is worth more
Than all the gold on Afric's shore.
One mite wrung from the labourer's hands
Shall buy and sell the miser's lands
Or, if protected from on high,
Does that whole nation sell and buy.
He who mocks the infant's faith
Shall be mock'd in Age and Death.
He who shall teach the child to doubt
The rotting grave shall ne'er get out.
He who respects the infant's faith
Triumphs over Hell and Death.
The child's toys and the old man's reasons
Are the fruits of the two seasons.
The questioner, who sits so sly,
Shall never know how to reply.
He who replies to words of Doubt
Doth put the light of knowledge out.
The strongest poison ever known
Came from Caesar's laurel crown.
Nought can deform the human race
Like to the armour's iron brace.
When gold and gems adorn the plough
To peaceful arts shall Envy bow.
A riddle, or the cricket's cry,

Is to Doubt a fit reply.
The emmet's inch and eagle's mile
Make lame Philosophy to smile.
He who doubts from what he sees
Will ne'er believe, do what you please.
If the Sun and Moon should doubt,
They'd immediately go out.
To be in a passion you good may do,
But no good if a passion is in you.
The whore and gambler, by the state
Licensed, build that nation's fate.
The harlot's cry from street to street
Shall weave Old England's winding–sheet.
The winner's shout, the loser's curse,
Dance before dead England's hearse.
Every night and every morn
Some to misery are born.
Every morn and every night
Some are born to sweet delight.
Some are born to sweet delight,
Some are born to endless night.
We are led to believe a lie
When we see not thro' the eye,
Which was born in a night, to perish in a night,
When the Soul slept in beams of light.
God appears, and God is Light,
To those poor souls who dwell in Night;
But does a Human Form display
To those who dwell in realms of Day.

Long John Brown and Little Mary Bell

Little Mary Bell had a Fairy in a nut,
Long John Brown had the Devil in his gut;
Long John Brown lov'd little Mary Bell,
And the Fairy drew the Devil into the nutshell.

Her Fairy skipp'd out and her Fairy skipp'd in;
He laugh'd at the Devil, saying `Love is a sin.'
The Devil he raged, and the Devil he was wroth,
And the Devil enter'd into the young man's broth.

He was soon in the gut of the loving young swain,
For John ate and drank to drive away love's pain;
But all he could do he grew thinner and thinner,
Tho' he ate and drank as much as ten men for his dinner.

Some said he had a wolf in his stomach day and night,
Some said he had the Devil, and they guess'd right;
The Fairy skipp'd about in his glory, joy and pride,
And he laugh'd at the Devil till poor John Brown died.

Then the Fairy skipp'd out of the old nutshell,
And woe and alack for pretty Mary Bell!
For the Devil crept in when the Fairy skipp'd out,
And there goes Miss Bell with her fusty old nut.

William Bond

I wonder whether the girls are mad,
And I wonder whether they mean to kill,
And I wonder if William Bond will die,
For assuredly he is very ill.

He went to church in a May morning,
Attended by Fairies, one, two, and three;
But the Angels of Providence drove them away,
And he return'd home in misery.

He went not out to the field nor fold,
He went not out to the village nor town,
But he came home in a black, black cloud,
And took to his bed, and there lay down.

And an Angel of Providence at his feet,
And an Angel of Providence at his head,
And in the midst a black, black cloud,
And in the midst the sick man on his bed.

And on his right hand was Mary Green,
And on his left hand was his sister Jane,
And their tears fell thro' the black, black cloud
To drive away the sick man's pain.

`O William, if thou dost another love,
Dost another love better than poor Mary,
Go and take that other to be thy wife,
And Mary Green shall her servant be.'

`Yes, Mary, I do another love,

THE PICKERING MANUSCRIPT

Another I love far better than thee,
And another I will have for my wife;
Then what have I to do with thee?

`For thou art melancholy pale,
And on thy head is the cold moon's shine,
But she is ruddy and bright as day,
And the sunbeams dazzle from her eyne.'

Mary trembled and Mary chill'd,
And Mary fell down on the right–hand floor,
That William Bond and his sister Jane
Scarce could recover Mary more.

When Mary woke and found her laid
On the right hand of her William dear,
On the right hand of his loved bed,
And saw her William Bond so near,

The Fairies that fled from William Bond
Danced around her shining head;
They danced over the pillow white,
And the Angels of Providence left the bed.

I thought Love lived in the hot sunshine,
But O, he lives in the moony light!
I thought to find Love in the heat of day,
But sweet Love is the comforter of night.

Seek Love in the pity of others' woe,
In the gentle relief of another's care,
In the darkness of night and the winter's snow,
In the naked and outcast, seek Love there!

9 781169 169244